# Welfare Reform in California

## State and County Implementation of CalWORKs in the Second Year

EXECUTIVE SUMMARY

Jacob Alex Klerman
Gail L. Zellman
Paul Steinberg

RAND **Statewide CalWORKs Evaluation**

Prepared for the California Department of Social Services

LABOR AND POPULATION

The research described in this report was prepared for the California Department of Social Services under Contract No. H38030.

ISBN: 0-8330-2881-2

RAND is a nonprofit institution that helps improve policy and decisionmaking through research and analysis. RAND® is a registered trademark. RAND's publications do not necessarily reflect the opinions or policies of its research sponsors.

Published 2001 by RAND
1700 Main Street, P.O. Box 2138, Santa Monica, CA 90407-2138
1200 South Hayes Street, Arlington, VA 22202-5050
RAND URL: http://www.rand.org/
To order RAND documents or to obtain additional information, contact Distribution Services: Telephone: (310) 451-7002; Fax: (310) 451-6915; Internet: order@rand.org

# PREFACE

In response to national welfare reform legislation—the Personal Responsibility and Work Opportunity Reconciliation Act (PRWORA), which was signed in August 1996—California passed legislation on August 11, 1997, that replaced the existing Aid to Families with Dependent Children (AFDC) and Greater Avenues for Independence (GAIN) programs with the California Work Opportunity and Responsibility to Kids (CalWORKs) program. Following an open and competitive bidding process, the California Department of Social Services (CDSS), which administers CalWORKs, awarded a contract to RAND to conduct a statewide evaluation of the CalWORKs program.

This RAND report presents an executive summary of the key findings from the second year of the process study component of the evaluation.

This document draws on the results of the main process analysis document, MR-1177-CDSS, *Welfare Reform in California: State and County Implementation of CalWORKs in the Second Year*, 2000.

For more information about the evaluation, see **http://www.rand.org/ CalWORKs** or contact:

Jacob Alex Klerman
RAND
1700 Main Street
P.O. Box 2138
Santa Monica, CA  90407-2138
(310) 393-0411 x6289
klerman@rand.org

Aris St. James
CDSS
744 P Street, MS 12-56
Sacramento, CA  98514

(916) 657-1959
astjames@dss.ca.gov

# CONTENTS

# FIGURES

# ACRONYMS

| | |
|---|---|
| ACIS | RAND's All-County Implementation Survey |
| AFDC | Aid to Families with Dependent Children |
| CalWORKs | California Work Opportunity and Responsibility to Kids Act of 1997 |
| CDSS | California Department of Social Services |
| CWD | County Welfare Department |
| GAIN | Greater Avenues for Independence (training program) |
| PRWORA | Personal Responsibility and Work Opportunity Reconciliation Act of 1996 |
| SIP | Self-initiated program |
| TANF | Temporary Assistance to Needy Families |
| WTW | Welfare-to-Work |

# 1. INTRODUCTION

## BACKGROUND

The Personal Responsibility and Work Opportunities Reconciliation Act of 1996 (PRWORA) fundamentally changed the American welfare system, replacing the Aid to Families with Dependent Children (AFDC) program with the Temporary Assistance for Needy Families (TANF) program. PRWORA deliberately and decisively shifted the authority to shape welfare programs from the federal government to the individual states. California's response to PRWORA was the California Work and Responsibility to Kids (CalWORKs) program—a "work-first" program that provides support services to help recipients move from welfare to work and toward self-sufficiency. To encourage prompt transitions to work and self-sufficiency, CalWORKs, like PRWORA, also imposes lifetime limits on the receipt of aid by adults. Finally, CalWORKs devolves much of the responsibility and authority for implementation to California's 58 counties, increasing counties' flexibility and financial accountability in designing their welfare programs.

*PRWORA fundamentally changed America's welfare system.*

*CalWORKs devolves responsibility to the counties.*

The California Department of Social Services (CDSS)—the state agency responsible for welfare—contracted with RAND for an independent evaluation of CalWORKs to assess both the process and the impact of the legislation, at both the state and county levels.

## OBJECTIVE

This report presents an executive summary of the results of RAND's analysis of the implementation of CalWORKs through the summer of 1999. The analysis relied on five sources of information:

*The analysis relied on five information sources.*

1. Field interviews—the primary method for collecting information—at the state level, intensively in six "focus counties" and less intensively in 18 "follow-up counties." Fieldwork in the counties involved interviews with upper management (senior County Welfare Department [CWD] and county officials) and line workers (e.g., office directors, supervisors, caseworkers), along with limited observation of field office facilities and CWD staff/recipient interactions.

2. Three mail survey efforts in August 1999: (1) the All County Implementation Survey (ACIS), completed by the CWD in each of the state's 58 counties; (2) a survey of non-CWD Alternative Payment Providers, who handle child-care payments; and (3) the CalWORKs Staffing Survey of approximately 150 caseworkers in each of the six focus counties and in 13 of the 18 follow-up counties.

3. Analyses of county data reported in official data systems, including caseloads (CA 237), aid payments (CA 237), expenses (CA 800, County Expense Form), the status of recipients in the Welfare-to-Work (WTW) program (GAIN 25/WTW 25), and receipt of aid (the MediCal Eligibility Determination System). In addition, some information from the six focus counties' individual-level eligibility and WTW data systems was used.

4. Review of written documents, including the CalWORKs legislation and the official regulations (CDSS's All-County Letters, County Fiscal Letters, and All-County Information Notices), the county plans, the county Notices of Action, county policies and procedures, and reports to boards of supervisors and senior CWD management.

5. Review of the secondary literature, including newspaper and magazine articles, government program reviews (e.g., those from the U.S. General Accounting Office), academic and policy literatures on welfare reform (e.g., Manpower Demonstration Research Corporation), and relevant public management and social science literatures.

In conducting the process analysis, RAND staff examined the legislative context for both the federal and California welfare reform legislation, reviewed the planning and budget process at the state level, analyzed the county-level process of gearing up to implement CalWORKs and the status of the implementation in the counties of WTW programs, and explored the implementation and delivery of services provided as part of CalWORKs (child care; transportation; education and training; mental health, substance abuse, and domestic abuse services; and child welfare).[1]

*Five key themes have emerged.*

This analysis revealed five key themes, which are developed in the following five sections:

- Despite declining caseloads, CWD workloads have increased (Section 2);

- CWDs have adopted different strategies to deal with this expanded workload (Section 3);

- The progress of recipients through the early steps of the WTW activities—appraisal, Job Club, and, as appropriate, assessment and post-assessment activities—to assessment has been slow (Section 4);

- Because the flow of recipients through the system has been slow and because many recipients have either found jobs or refused to participate in earlier activities, few recipients are in post-assessment activities (Section 5);

---

[1]See the main process analysis document, *Welfare Reform in California: State and County Implementation of CalWORKs in the Second Year, 2000*, MR-1177-CDSS, for more detail on each of these analysis areas.

- Referrals to education and training and to treatment for mental health, substance abuse, and domestic abuse have been low (Section 6).

Finally, given these five themes, Section 7 discusses issues for further consideration as the CalWORKs implementation continues to evolve.

## 2. DESPITE A DECLINING CASELOAD, THE CWD WORKLOAD HAS INCREASED

Between the passage of PRWORA in August 1996 and the passage of CalWORKs in August 1997, California's welfare caseload declined by 18 percent from its peak in July 1995, and it continued to decline in many counties by about 1 percent a month.

*California's welfare caseload has declined.*

Given this declining caseload, many observers, including members of the boards of supervisors in many counties, assumed that the CWD workload would decrease commensurately and therefore that CWD staffing levels could be reduced. While this assumption was natural, it was incorrect, primarily because, compared with AFDC/GAIN, the CalWORKs model implies a much more intensive approach to service delivery—one that requires a significantly higher workload per case. It appears that this higher workload per case more than offsets any decrease in the workload resulting from the declining caseload.

*Higher workload per case offsets the benefits of the caseload decline.*

In this section, we examine this finding in more detail, focusing on the effects of this higher workload per case, first in the intermediate term and then in the short term.

### HIGHER WORKLOAD PER CASE INCREASED WORKLOAD IN THE INTERMEDIATE TERM

In the long run, implementation of CalWORKs may lead to workload decreases as the caseload declines, either because the services help recipients find jobs and leave aid or because recipients reach time limits and became ineligible for aid. However, in the intermediate term, the workload per case under CalWORKs is higher, more than compensating for the decline in the number of cases (see Figure 2.1). This increase in the intermediate-term workload derives from three interrelated factors: First, the CalWORKs model involves expanded WTW services for an expanded set of recipients. Second, this expansion in the WTW program has indirectly increased the volume of eligibility tasks. Finally, the CalWORKs legislation imposed new eligibility tasks.

*Increase in the intermediate-term workload stems from three factors.*

#### The Impact of Expanding WTW Services

Based on our analysis, the intermediate-term per-case WTW workload should have been expected to increase sharply, perhaps to double, solely to provide the expanded WTW services that were a part of CalWORKs. Unlike the Greater Avenues for Independence (GAIN) program that it replaced, CalWORKs was intended to provide WTW programs to a much larger share of the welfare population. While GAIN had been a

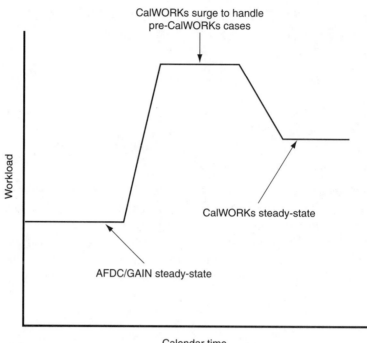

**Figure 2.1—Increase in the Short- and Intermediate-Term WTW Workload**

small program, serving less than one-quarter of the caseload, CalWORKs was to be nearly universal. Along with the mandate to serve nearly every adult recipient, funding increased sharply.

*Compared with GAIN, CalWORKs has expanded the scope of services.*

Specifically, under CalWORKs, exemption criteria were narrowed and minimum hours of participation were required. Under GAIN, parents with children under three years of age were exempted from participation in WTW programs, whereas under CalWORKs, the exemption was narrowed to no more than one year (less, at county discretion). And those who did participate were required to participate nearly full-time—by July 1999, 32 hours per week. Increases in work requirements, in turn, expanded the need for support services such as child care and transportation, and funds were provided.

Furthermore, unlike the GAIN model, which often involved long education assignments, the CalWORKs work-first model involves relatively short WTW assignments. Job Club lasts from four days to four weeks; enrolling in short-term vocational training is more consistent with the CalWORKs model than enrolling in long-term degree programs at community colleges. These shorter assignments increase the case management burden, as caseworkers are expected to refer clients to multiple activities over time and to monitor participation more closely.

In addition, the scope of services under CalWORKs was expanded to include post-employment services, so recipients who got jobs were no longer automatically deregistered from WTW, and those who left aid continued to be eligible for some services.

Finally, beyond the statutory high participation-rate requirements, time limits have imparted a sense of urgency. More labor-intensive case management is needed to use the limited time on aid effectively.

*Time limits impose a sense of urgency.*

### The Impact of WTW Expansion on Eligibility Operations

The expanded WTW program also has had important indirect effects on eligibility operations. County line staff report that the workload for cases in which an adult is working is two to three times that for cases in which no adult is working. The grant for nonworking cases is usually unchanged from month to month; for working cases, earnings often fluctuate from month to month (and within months), requiring recomputation of the grant. The continued robust economic expansion in the state and the phasing-in of the CalWORKs programs have resulted in increased employment among the remaining recipients, so that by mid-1999, about 30 percent of adult recipients were working. If the program succeeds in helping more recipients find and keep jobs, the eligibility workload per case will continue to increase.

*Increased employment leads to a higher eligibility workload per case.*

Furthermore, with many more recipients required to participate in WTW activities under CalWORKs, more of them are noncompliant and more sanctions need to be processed. This, in turn, leads to more eligibility operations.

### The Impact of New Eligibility Tasks

During the original CalWORKs debate in 1997, there was serious discussion of eligibility simplification in general. Nevertheless, no eligibility simplification was implemented, and the final CalWORKs legislation included additional eligibility tasks. The CWD was now expected to verify that children were attending school and that they were properly immunized as part of its ongoing eligibility function. Furthermore, CWD staff, including eligibility workers, were to screen for, and make referrals to, new services—mental health, substance abuse, and domestic abuse services.

*CalWORKs introduced new eligibility tasks.*

### THE EFFECTS ON WORKLOAD IN THE SHORT TERM WERE EVEN MORE SEVERE

In the short term, the impact on workload was even more severe, because in addition to processing *new* cases through the steps of the CalWORKs model, CWDs were expected to process the *existing* (pre-CalWORKs) caseload through those same steps. On average, across the state, there are about three times as many recipients at a given point in time as there

*CWDs must process both new and existing cases.*

are new cases in a year; therefore, processing the pre-CalWORKs cases required major efforts by CWDs.

*Processing existing cases creates a "pig in the python" problem.*

This need to process the pre-CalWORKs cases induced a "pig in the python" problem. While the intermediate-term per-case workload under CalWORKs was likely to be higher than that for new cases under AFDC/GAIN, the short-term per-case workload was likely to be higher still, as illustrated conceptually in Figure 2.1. Since in the short term, changes in the size of the caseload were small compared with changes in the per-case workload, the total workload also followed the path displayed in Figure 2.1. If the CWD tried to process all the pre-CalWORKs cases in a year, the total short-term workload would perhaps be twice as high as the steady-state under CalWORKs (which was itself perhaps twice as high as the AFDC/GAIN steady-state).

*The short-term workload surge was a major management challenge.*

This short-term surge in the workload was a major management challenge for the CWDs. On the one hand, the ticking time-limit clocks of existing recipients argued for moving existing and new cases through the steps of the CalWORKs model as quickly as possible. On the other hand, it was simply not possible to process all the pre-CalWORKs cases instantaneously. The size of the surge suggested that it was prudent to try to spread the workload of processing the existing cases over a longer period of time—a year or more.

## 3. CWDs MADE DIFFERENT CAPACITY-BUILDING DECISIONS TO DEAL WITH THE EXPANDED WORKLOAD

For CWDs, this increase in the workload was problematic. They had barely enough capacity—e.g., staff and contractors—to handle the pre-CalWORKs workload. The caseload decline in the second half of the 1990s merely unwound the increase in the caseload in the first half of that decade. The earlier increase had occurred at a time when the state and its counties were in the midst of a major fiscal crisis. As a result, most counties had not increased their staffing levels proportionately with the increase in the caseload. Thus, the decline in the caseload merely brought per-worker caseloads back to their "normal" levels of the early 1990s.

*CWDs had barely enough capacity for the pre-CalWORKs workload.*

CalWORKs would significantly increase the workload, which meant that the counties had to decide how to manage the workload over time. Counties made both *tactical* decisions—what to do first and what to defer—and longer-term *strategic* decisions—whether and how to increase capacity. The CWDs had three strategies available: outsourcing, adding CWD staff, and "toughing it out." Counties following the toughing-it-out strategy chose not to hire new staff or to outsource, but rather to work slowly through the caseload with existing capacity.

*CWDs had three strategies for dealing with the rising workload.*

In this section, we examine county decisions to increase capacity through outsourcing and adding CWD staff.

### OUTSOURCING VARIED WIDELY ACROSS THE COUNTIES

Some counties sought to increase capacity by contracting with other agencies to provide some set of CalWORKs services (e.g., job search/Job Club, assessment, case management). The scope of outsourcing varied widely, with some counties (e.g., San Diego and Kern) outsourcing many of their core WTW operations, and others (e.g., Contra Costa, El Dorado, Nevada, Riverside, Santa Clara, Tulare, and Ventura) outsourcing none of the core WTW activities.

*The scope of out-sourcing varied widely . . .*

Strategies for outsourcing also varied by which WTW activities were outsourced. For example, 14 of our 24 study counties outsourced Job Club, either as a discrete activity or as part of a larger package of WTW services. In addition, because assessment is a specialized function requiring special training in test administration and interpretation of scores, as well as current knowledge of the local job market, many counties that kept most operations in-house outsourced assessment. Finally, because post-employment case management was not a part of GAIN, it

*. . . as did strategies for outsourcing.*

was new for CWDs, and thus there was considerable uncertainty about the demand for it; in many counties, it was outsourced. In addition, many CWDs also recognized that they had little in-house expertise in providing post-employment services.

Finally, counties varied in their choice of organizations to which they outsourced their services. ACIS results show that when CWDs outsourced, they usually turned to other government agencies and to non-profits (often community-based organizations) and only infrequently to for-profit corporations.

*Outsourcing variation was driven by diverse considerations.*

What was outsourced, where it was outsourced, and to whom it was outsourced appear to have been driven by a diverse set of considerations, including supplier availability—a particular issue for smaller counties where willing and able contractors were often not available—and whether the CWDs had the capabilities in-house to provide services that required specially trained employees and that were far from the core mission of the CWD. These services—which included education and training, substance abuse and mental health treatment, and domestic abuse counseling—were often outsourced.

Ideological, labor, and political considerations also played a crucial role. Some counties had a strong pro-private-sector orientation that encouraged outsourcing, while others were strongly anti-outsourcing.

*Previous experience strongly influenced outsourcing decisions.*

Finally, previous experience had a strong influence on whether to outsource. For example, counties that had work-first programs in place before CalWORKs often chose to simply expand them. These past experiences pushed in different directions. Riverside County continued its practice of not outsourcing WTW activities; Los Angeles County continued to outsource orientation, Job Club, and assessment. However, for many counties, simply continuing their pre-CalWORKs relationships was not an option. Most counties did not have significant work-first/Job Club GAIN programs on which to build. Moreover, many counties that had some program in place considered that program to be unsuccessful or inappropriate for CalWORKs and chose not to extend it. In counties without successful outsourcing contracts in place, recipients usually did not start receiving services until six months to a year after the outsourcing decision was made.

## ADDING STAFF WAS A TIME-CONSUMING PROCESS FOR COUNTIES

*Hiring staff was an alternative strategy.*

An alternative strategy for adding capacity was to hire additional staff. However, for counties that chose this option, new staff were not available immediately. Hiring required receiving explicit permission from the Board of Supervisors, posting the job, and then interviewing, hiring, and training the new employees (both formal training and a probationary period were required). In addition, appropriate space, furniture, and office equipment needed to be acquired and installed. In many counties, expedited civil service hiring procedures were available and were followed, but even so, the process required nearly a year in most cases.

Hiring timelines were lengthened by the practice of upgrading current staff. New positions were often filled by CWD employees from lower pay grades; as the new positions were filled, lower-level slots became vacant, requiring backfilling. County hiring procedures usually prevented CWDs from backfilling in parallel with the initial hiring. Counties that did extensive hiring (e.g., Alameda) reported that the backfilling was still going on as of the summer of 1999.

*Hiring from within lengthened the process . . .*

The practice of hiring from within was the subject of considerable discussion. It was to be expected that some of the new positions would be filled by previous CWD employees, since they knew of the openings, knew something about the way the system worked, and preferred working for county government and with welfare recipients. Nevertheless, many observers expressed concern about the degree of hiring from within. Many of the new job-specialist positions have very different job descriptions than the eligibility-worker positions from which people came. Some counties (e.g., Sacramento and Stanislaus) formally waived the minimum qualifications or allowed new job specialists to acquire the required education over a grace period of several years. In addition, the ranking process in some counties gave points for county service.

*. . . and raised concerns about the positions filled this way.*

Both county and state observers expressed concern that the net effect of these hiring procedures was that better-qualified, outside candidates were ignored in favor of internal candidates. Instead of hiring outside people with the qualifications for the less-structured job-specialist positions, counties simply promoted eligibility workers into these occupations. Many informed observers expressed concern that these internal candidates did not have the training, the education, or possibly even the temperament for their new positions.

Not surprisingly, the process has not always gone smoothly. Observers in San Francisco County reported that at least one-quarter of those selected for new combined worker positions early in the CalWORKs implementation process voluntarily chose to return to their previous positions very quickly. Those who left generally said the new job was too demanding; others who stayed appear to be performing well.

*The hiring process has not always gone smoothly.*

However, current CWD employees were an available labor source in a tight labor market, and hiring from outside was often difficult. In the 1999 ACIS, 30 of the 58 counties (58 percent) reported that the lack of qualified applicants for caseworker positions had hindered their implementation of CalWORKs. In a hot labor market, CWD jobs are often viewed as not the most desirable among those available, and in the CalWORKs environment, such jobs are quite challenging. One CWD director said, "The cream of the crop [people who pass the civil service test] go to private enterprise, which pays more."

*Reclassification studies posed an additional hurdle.*

In some counties, hiring timelines were further lengthened by organizational changes in response to reform. Counties that chose to redesign the jobs performed faced an additional hurdle. In a civil service environment, these new positions and even new responsibilities triggered a need for a "reclassification study"—a formal review of job qualifications, the creation of a new job classification, and usually an increase in the pay scale. About one-third of all counties (18 of the 58 counties) reported in the 1999 ACIS that they had reclassified caseworker positions, another six counties had reclassification studies under way, and 12 counties were considering reclassifying positions. In some counties, hiring could not proceed until the reclassification study was completed. Thus, these studies further delayed the process of hiring new staff to deal with the increased workload.

# 4. THE FLOW OF CASES HAS BEEN SLOW

While CWDs were putting in place the capacity to meet the increased workload, they simultaneously had to begin moving their mandatory WTW caseloads through the early steps of the CalWORKs process model: enrollment/orientation/appraisal; job search/Job Club; assessment; signing the WTW plan; and post-assessment WTW activities. One of the key questions the process analysis seeks to answer is, How slowly or quickly are the participants moving through these steps? According to the analysis, the pace of implementation through the pre-assessment part of the model—orientation/appraisal and job search/Job Club—has been slow.

*CWDs also had to move caseloads through early CalWORKs steps.*

The slow pace of implementation is not particularly surprising. As discussed in detail in last year's process analysis,[2] from the beginning, the late passage of the legislation delayed the actual implementation of CalWORKs. California was one of the last states to pass welfare reform legislation after the passage of PRWORA, but for recipients, the state's 60-month time clock began ticking as of January 1998. CWDs have scrambled to develop and implement programs to make recipients self-sufficient before the time limits are reached. Whatever problems counties have encountered in doing this quickly were, in turn, exacerbated by the need to build up capacity to handle what has turned out to be an expanding workload, as described in Sections 2 and 3.

*The slow pace is not that surprising.*

In this section, we discuss the slow pace of implementation, starting first with a big-picture view of the problem and then considering the problem at the county level.

## THE ACTUAL FLOW OF CASES IS SLOWER THAN WHAT IS POSSIBLE

In thinking about the flow of participants through the initial phase of the mandated steps, it is useful to consider the possible pace versus the actual pace: how long it could take from approval of the application for aid to the first WTW activity versus how long it has actually taken. Figure 4.1 shows two timelines.

---

[2]*Welfare Reform in California: State and County Implementation of CalWORKs in the First Year, 1999*, RAND, MR-1051-CDSS, 1999.

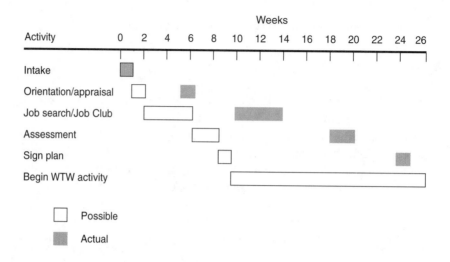

**Figure 4.1—Time to First WTW Activity: Possible and Actual**

### The Possible Pace of Implementation

*Moving compliant new cases through to a signed plan in ten weeks is possible.*

How fast could a county move a participant through the steps described above, from intake (approval of the application) to a signed WTW plan?[3] The open bars in Figure 4.1 show an idealized schedule for moving a participant from approval to a signed WTW plan in less than ten weeks (at least one county has such a ten-week goal). In this idealized flow, orientation and appraisal take place in the week following approval of the application for aid. Somewhere in the two weeks after approval, any needed child care and transportation are arranged. The four weeks of job search/Job Club begin the following Monday—that is, the Monday of week 3—and last through Friday of week 6. For those who do not find a job through Job Club/job search, an assessment is conducted in week 7. Week 8 is devoted to scoring any tests administered during the assessment. A WTW plan is developed and signed at a meeting in week 9, and the first WTW activity begins on the following Monday (i.e., week 10).

---

[3]This analysis applies only to a specific case: a compliant participant with no serious barriers to participation who encounters no problems. It thus excludes any recipients who are prescreened and assigned to some initial activity other than Job Club (e.g., a self-initiated program [SIP], remedial education, behavioral health treatment). It also excludes the large fraction (perhaps one-third to one-half) of recipients who are noncompliant at some point at or before the first post-assessment WTW activity. Finally, it excludes willing recipients who experience the day-to-day crises that are part of the lives of welfare recipients: child-care problems, car problems, sick children, own illness, etc. Thus, even in smoothly running programs with a ten-week goal, most participants will not reach the first post-assessment WTW activity by ten weeks, or even 15 or 20 weeks.

## The Actual Pace of Implementation

In practice, however, the actual time through the steps is quite a bit longer in many counties (as shown notionally by the gray bars in Figure 4.1). While the lengths of the bars—i.e., the amounts of time actually spent in each step—are not all that different from those of the idealized case, the lags between steps are dramatically different. As shown, there is a lag of about a month between steps, and this appears to be the reality in some counties. The consequence of such lags is that while the first post-assessment WTW activity for an uncomplicated, compliant participant could start in week 10, or earlier, participants are often just starting Job Club at that point. Moreover, subsequent lags mean that the finished WTW plan is not even signed until week 26 or later—a full half-year (or more) after approval.

*The actual pace is slower . . .*

*. . . often because of lags between steps.*

In practice, time to Job Club is often longer because of recipient non-compliance and special barriers. However, in some counties, capacity constraints and coordination difficulties appear to drive the lags in the gray bars and make achieving the idealized schedule difficult. The schedule depicted by the open bars implicitly assumes that there is sufficient capacity for each required appointment to be available in the following week and that programs (e.g., Job Club, post-assessment WTW activities) begin each Monday. In addition, in the idealized schedule, it must be possible for appraisal to take place early enough in the week immediately following approval to allow the recipient to arrange child care; it must be possible for assessment to occur in the week immediately following Job Club; and it must be possible for the first post-assessment WTW activity to begin in the week immediately following the signing of the WTW plan.

*Capacity and coordination difficulties drive the lags.*

## COUNTIES FALL INTO THREE GROUPS IN MOVING PARTICIPANTS THROUGH THE STEPS

The gray bars in Figure 4.1 represent the typical experience described in our interviews. However, county experiences vary. Our analysis shows that the counties fall into three distinct groups: (1) those that had large GAIN programs or successful, flexible contracts in place prior to CalWORKs; (2) those that did not have large or flexible programs in place but succeeded in quickly adding capacity; and (3) those that did not have large or flexible programs in place and did not quickly add capacity or underestimated the workload.

*Counties varied in how quickly they ramped up.*

The counties in the first group often ramped up quickly, putting sufficient capacity in place before the end of 1998 and moving the bulk of their caseload through appraisal, Job Club, and assessment by mid-1999.

The counties in the second group were not so favorably situated. While they moved promptly to add capacity, new contracts did not yield that new capacity until early 1999. Hiring and then backfilling positions vacated when lower-level employees moved into the newly created positions took even longer. Enrollment was not completed until (or in a few cases after) the December 31, 1998, statutory deadline, and appraisal did not begin in volume until the fall of 1998 and did not reach the steady-state level until the spring of 1999. Job Club began in volume about the same time, but was still continuing at well above the steady-state level as of late summer 1999 and seemed likely to continue at least through the end of the year. Assessment and signing of WTW plans (for the non-employed) began in volume in early 1999 and seemed likely to continue in volume well above the steady-state level into 2000.

The counties in the third group, apparently including many of the larger ones, either did not act promptly, underestimated the workload, or encountered other problems. At the end of summer 1999, they had large backlogs of cases awaiting Job Club, and it seemed unlikely that the Job Club surge would end before 2000. For many recipients, assessment, signing WTW plans, and post-assessment would occur after that.

## 5. FEW PARTICIPANTS ARE MOVING INTO POST-ASSESSMENT STEPS

The analysis presented above describes the pace of implementation, but it does not answer another key process analysis question: What is the status of the participants? That is, where are they in the CalWORKs process model? Although moving participants through the steps—both the steps up through assessment and the post-assessment steps—of the Cal-WORKs process model is the focus of CWDs in implementing Cal-WORKs, our analysis revealed that only about one-quarter of the mandatory participants are actually within these core steps and less than half of them are in the post-assessment steps. Taking a linear view of the Cal-WORKs process model, one would expect participants to move into the post-assessment steps once they have moved through the steps up through assessment. However, the CalWORKs process model is nonlinear, as reflected in the fact that there are two alternative "exit" routes to linear movement through the core steps. According to our analysis, the majority of participants are exiting the core steps before assessment through two common alternative routes—noncompliance and employment.

*Less than one-quarter of participants are in core steps . . .*

*. . . with most exiting before assessment.*

This section discusses the distribution of the mandatory caseload through the overall CalWORKs process model and the concerns for counties raised by those participants who are in either of the two alternative exit routes.

### PARTICIPANTS ARE DISTRIBUTED ACROSS THE CORE STEPS AND TWO EXIT ROUTES

Figure 5.1 summarizes the key aspects of the CalWORKs program model, with the core steps represented by the boxes running down the center of the figure. We divide the figure into four areas: The top area (above the horizontal line)—the initial phase of the implementation process—includes the set of steps that should apply to most cases shortly after their application for aid is approved. The sequence of steps in this initial phase begins with the approval of the application, proceeds to orientation to CalWORKs and its WTW services and appraisal, and then proceeds to Job Club. For those who do not find a job through Job Club, assessment follows, and then a WTW plan is signed. This flow represents the steps through assessment.

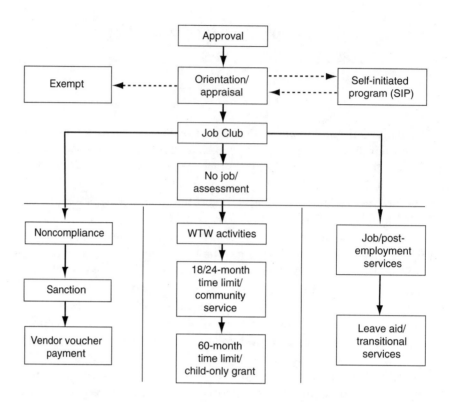

**Figure 5.1—The CalWORKs Process Model**

*Signing the WTW plan begins a second phase.*

With the signing of a WTW plan, the initial phase ends and the second phase begins (in the center of Figure 5.1, below the horizontal line). A participant should now begin a sequence of WTW activities designed to overcome barriers to employment (e.g., subsidized work; education and training; or mental health, substance abuse, and domestic violence services) and thus allow him or her to find work and ultimately leave aid. Until work is found, the recipient repeats cycles of reassessment (formally known as reappraisal), a revised WTW work plan, and a new WTW activity. If the recipient has not found employment by the 18/24-month time limit (from the signing of the WTW plan), he or she is then given a mandatory assignment to community service. Unless employment is found, the recipient continues in community service through the end of his or her 60-month lifetime limit. At that point, the aid payment is reduced by the adult portion of the recipient's grant.

However, signing a WTW plan and beginning a WTW activity is not the only way to leave the initial phase. The left and right columns below the horizontal line in Figure 5.1 represent other, more common exit routes from the initial phase, noncompliance and employment.

*Noncompliance is one way to exit the initial phase.*

CWDs report that between one-third and two-thirds of all participants instructed to attend any activity fail to do so. Figure 5.1 shows noncompliance occurring at Job Club, where it is common; but noncompliance also occurs at most other points in the program. The CalWORKs legislation specifies procedures for dealing with such noncompliance. First, a Notice of Action for noncompliance is sent; this is followed by a formal conciliation process; and finally, a financial sanction eliminates the non-complying adult from the case for the purposes of computing the grant.

Alternatively, many recipients find employment. Some are employed at the time of application for aid; some find employment before Job Club; and others find employment during Job Club. Work is their WTW activity, and the next steps for these participants are voluntary post-employment services designed to keep them employed and to move them toward better jobs, with the aim of helping them to move off aid and achieve self-sufficiency. According to the final regulations, as long as they are working the required 32 hours per week, participants in this group do not need to sign a WTW plan.

*Employment is another way . . .*

Other ways to leave the initial phase are represented by the dotted arrows at the top of Figure 5.1. The arrows and box to the left refer to those recipients who are exempted for good cause from participation during orientation; those whose WTW activity is mental health or substance abuse treatment, so they are not required to attend Job Club; or those who are screened out for learning disability reasons or behavioral health problems. The arrows and box to the right refer to those who are participating in preexisting education or training programs known as self-initiated programs (SIPs). In addition, some recipients leave aid within a few months of approval. Many of them never proceed beyond this initial phase.

*. . . while exemptions are a third way.*

What is the status of the participants in terms of this model? Using tabulations from the September 1999 WTW 25 forms filed by the CWDs, we can construct a "snapshot." Although the data on the WTW 25 forms suffer from missing information and are sometimes of questionable quality, we can adjust to account partially for these problems.

These tabulations suggest that about 26 percent of the counties' mandatory WTW cases are within the core steps of the CalWORKs process: About 14 percent are in the initial phase—appraisal (7.4 percent), job search (5.2 percent), and assessment (1.7 percent)—and about 12 percent are in a post-assessment WTW activity. In addition, about 20 percent of the mandatory cases are in the formal noncompliance process (i.e., have received a noncompliance Notice of Action), while about 31 percent are working. Another 11 percent are in some form of exemption.

*26 percent of the cases are within core steps . . .*

The remainder—nearly 29 percent (after adjusting for double counting in the separate counts listed above)—are unaccounted for (because participants can be in multiple activities, the figures do not sum). In other words, they have not been exempted or sanctioned, but they are not in any activity. Where are these participants? They appear to fall into three groups: (1) those awaiting Job Club or assessment; (2) those between

*. . . and nearly 29 percent are unaccounted for within the system.*

20

post-assessment WTW activities; and (3) those who are noncompliant, but for whom the CWDs have not yet begun formal noncompliance procedures.

## NONCOMPLIANCE IS A SERIOUS PROBLEM FOR THE COUNTIES

*Counties report high no-show rates . . .*

With about 20 percent of the caseload in formal noncompliance status, noncompliance is a serious problem. Every county reports high rates of no-shows. Most counties report that for any given activity, between one-third and two-thirds of participants fail to attend when instructed to do so. The problem is most salient at Job Club, but it appears to occur at each step and in most counties.

*. . . but even these rates understate the problem.*

Even the 20 percent noncompliance rate understates the level of noncompliance with WTW activities. As mentioned above, many of the unaccounted-for participants are actually noncompliant cases who have not yet received Notices of Action and therefore are not counted on the WTW 25 form as "noncompliant." This group includes recipients who did not participate in an activity and either have not yet been contacted about their noncompliance or have agreed to come into compliance but have not yet done so.

*There are three reasons for non-compliance.*

While the problem of noncompliance is clear, the reasons for it are less clear. Our analysis suggests three reasons. The first stems from participant fears of participating in a WTW step (usually Job Club). The second reason is willful noncompliance—recipients simply choose not to participate, perhaps because they are already working "under the table" and participation (e.g., Job Club) would force them to forfeit the job. The third reason, CWD deficiencies, includes such things as recipients not receiving or understanding notices, scheduling conflicts (e.g., for recipients working part-time), and recipients having either easily remediable but unaddressed barriers to participation (e.g., being unaware that the CWD will pay for child care) or serious but unrecognized barriers to participation (e.g., learning disabilities).

*Home visits can address the non-compliance problem.*

Counties report that home visits—which many counties are implementing or piloting—are a potentially useful, if expensive, strategy for dealing with noncompliance. Home visits provide a natural vehicle for motivating compliance among the reluctant and fearful. Observers also claim that the interaction between a CWD staff person and recipients during such home visits can help identify and address CWD deficiencies. Finally, home visits provide an opportunity to identify fraud—to determine, for example, that the recipients are not available for a home visit because they are working, that the children supposedly receiving aid are not present, or that other adults appear to be living in the household. A large home visit program in San Bernardino County appears to be having some success at bringing recipients into compliance. However, home visits are viewed by some as overly intrusive and have been opposed by advocates.

When recipients do not comply, the CalWORKs legislation provides for the use of sanctions, which cut recipient benefits. Given the consistently high reported rates of no-shows to early CalWORKs activities and the provisions of the CalWORKs legislation, one would expect high sanction rates. However, those rates tend to be lower than expected, given the high rates of noncompliance. At the beginning of CalWORKs, many counties were simply too busy dealing with the compliant cases to sanction the noncompliant cases, and even now, some counties (and many managers and individual caseworkers) are extremely reluctant to sanction, preferring to encourage participation.

*Sanction rates are lower than expected.*

## HIGH LEVELS OF EMPLOYMENT ARE A DESIRED PROGRAM GOAL BUT ALSO AN ONGOING CHALLENGE

Although noncompliance—an undesired program outcome—is high, employment—a desired program outcome—is also high: Almost one-third of the recipients in the state are working. However, most of their jobs do not increase income enough to move them off aid—the ultimate program goal. To meet this goal, counties can provide post-employment services, such as job retention, job advancement, and case management services.

There are two key challenges to delivering post-employment services: First, counties must determine which post-employment services to offer, if any, and they must decide whether to provide assistance to all Cal-WORKs clients who become employed or just to those employed clients who remain on aid. Of our 24 study counties, 19 offer post-employment services, with most focused on providing case management (ongoing contact with recipients above and beyond what is required to compute and issue the welfare benefit), and many were still in the pilot stage as of fall 1999. A recent randomized experiment suggests that such case management strategies have no measurable effect on employment or exits from aid. Education and training are an alternative strategy, but it is not clear how to combine these activities with work. Second, as long as participants are meeting their 32-hour participation requirement, they are not required to attend post-employment services. Counties find it difficult to engage employed CalWORKs clients in such services, and they report that demand for them is low.

*Delivering post-employment services raises two challenges.*

## 6. THE NUMBER OF REFERRALS TO CalWORKs SERVICES HAS BEEN LOW

Unlike GAIN, the CalWORKs legislation describes and provides additional funding for a range of services for welfare recipients—child care, transportation, education and training, and behavioral health services (mental health, alcohol and substance abuse, and domestic abuse services). Although there was a belief that such conditions were common and that referrals to these services would be high, the number of such referrals has been low.

While the small number of referrals has been of concern to observers in CDSS, in the CWDs, and in the provider and advocate communities, it should not be surprising, given the work-first orientation of the CalWORKs legislation and start-up issues. In the pure work-first model of CalWORKs, referrals to services should be expected to occur later in the WTW process, at the time of the assessment, rather than up front, at the time of appraisal.

*The small number of referrals stems partly from CalWORKs' work-first orientation.*

### COUNTIES HAVE A WORK-FIRST FOCUS, ALTHOUGH IT IS NOT *PURE* WORK-FIRST

The CalWORKs legislation has work-first features, including its any-employment-first goal. To that end, unless specifically exempted, all recipients are to begin job search immediately following approval of their application for aid. From this pure work-first perspective, pre-job-search activities—orientation and a pre-job-search appraisal—need only deliver the work-first message and ensure that participants have child care and transportation to enable them to work. According to a pure work-first philosophy, before job search there is little reason to screen for barriers to work (e.g., learning disabilities or substance abuse, mental health, or domestic violence problems) or to provide services to address those barriers.

*Employment is the first goal under CalWORKs . . .*

The reason for such minimal pre-screening follows directly from a pure work-first philosophy, as expressed by several of our interviewees. In a pure work-first program, services are provided only to make people employable, and the labor market is viewed as the best test of employability. Some people who might have been deemed clearly employable by a CWD *will not* find jobs; others deemed clearly not employable *will* find jobs. Rather than trying to predict who will not find a job, caseworkers simply send everyone to job search. According to this work-first philosophy, people who find a job have revealed that they do not need the services. Only those who do not find a job "need" services, and therefore

*. . . which implies minimal up-front screening.*

only they should be referred to services. As one respondent noted, "People work with drug problems everywhere."

*CalWORKs programs are growing less work-first over time.*

Neither the CalWORKs legislation nor county CalWORKs implementations are pure work-first programs. As illustrated by the top part of Figure 5.1, exemptions and referrals can and do occur before Job Club, at the appraisal stage. CalWORKs grew out of the GAIN program, which had strong human-capital-development roots, and it gives considerable discretion to the counties in designing their programs. In addition, it appears that county CalWORKs programs are, in practice, becoming less pure work-first over time, although they are still very different from the human-capital-development efforts that characterized early GAIN programs.

This change appears to be the result of several different and only weakly related forces. First, the legislation clearly allows for, provides funding for, and in many cases requires extensive and expensive services to help those with barriers to work to enter the labor force. Second, subsequent regulatory efforts have reinforced the modified work-first aspects of the legislation (e.g., ensuring the availability of the SIP option and adult basic education for learning disabilities and non-English speakers as a WTW activity). Third, the formal and informal urging of CDSS has been a contributing force. Given this urging, some counties (e.g., Los Angeles, for substance abuse) have begun screening more intensively for barriers to work before sending recipients to Job Club. Fourth, pressure from service providers, who are receiving far fewer referrals than expected, often seems to have contributed to such changes. Fifth, in some counties, advocates have strongly urged such changes. Sixth, county CalWORKs programs are maturing, so management has more time to develop and refine pre-screening programs.

## STILL, COUNTIES REMAIN WORK-FIRST FOCUSED, AS REFLECTED BY LOW REFERRALS

*Less than 7 percent of the cases statewide have been referred prior to Job Club.*

Despite these options and the formal and informal urging from CDSS, the CalWORKs programs in most counties remain relatively close to a pure work-first model. Using the adjusted September WTW 25 data, we find that few cases are being pulled out before Job Club for alternative activities. Statewide, less than 7 percent of participants are in adult basic education, are receiving behavioral health services (treatment for substance abuse or mental health), or are in SIPs for education. Moreover, more than half of those cases appear to be SIPs, for which, by statute, the recipient must have been involved in the educational program before appraisal.

These results are consistent with a relatively pure work-first perspective in which services are to be provided only to make recipients employable and with the realization that CalWORKs staff can only imperfectly identify those who would not find a job through Job Club. Referrals to these alternative activities should, therefore, be expected to occur primarily as barriers are identified in Job Club and at assessment after failure to find a job. Insofar as this analysis is correct, we would expect the number of referrals to be determined by the flow of cases through Job Club and assessment and the rates at which assessed cases are referred. Consistent with this analysis, the limited available data suggest that referrals rise sharply as cases flow into Job Club and assessment.

# 7. ISSUES FOR FURTHER CONSIDERATION

As the counties' CalWORKs programs continue to mature in the coming year, a series of issues remain worthy of further consideration. We raise these issues and, when appropriate, discuss potentially promising ways to address them.

## COMBINING ELIGIBILITY AND WTW OPERATIONS

The implementation of CalWORKs provided CWDs with the opportunity to reorganize, particularly in terms of how they combine eligibility and WTW operations. Counties have generally chosen either to keep the operations separate (as was usually the case under GAIN) or to completely merge them (assigning both eligibility and WTW responsibilities to a single worker). Some counties report success with each approach. Our fieldwork suggests some concerns about choosing either extreme. Keeping the operations separate means that there is a need for handoffs between workers and multiple appointments for recipients, which means there are opportunities for participants to "fall through the cracks" or at least for delays due to the need for separate appointments. While merging operations reduces handoffs, it raises another concern: The combined job may simply be too big. Some observers report that the deadlines of eligibility tasks push out WTW tasks. Others report that those with the temperament for one task are less suitable for the other task.

*Counties have chosen extremes in combining eligibility and WTW operations.*

Instead, some intermediate approach may be preferable. Such an approach might include having a single pre-Job Club worker who keeps those tasks that can be easily done by an individual and assigns those jobs requiring specialized knowledge to a separate specialized worker, or combining separate workers under a single supervisor or program manager.

## OUTCOMES-BASED MANAGEMENT

CalWORKs represents a fundamental change in the CWD mission. Under AFDC, the CWD's primary task was the correct computation of the grants. Under CalWORKs, this task has not gone away; however, the importance of another task—helping almost all recipients become employed, achieve self-sufficiency, and leave cash aid—has increased greatly. This latter task had been present under GAIN, but under CalWORKs the share of recipients affected has increased sharply and the scope of effort has broadened.

*CalWORKs entails fundamental change in the CWD mission.*

*Mission change implies a shift in management strategy . . .*

This change implies a fundamental shift in management strategy. Now, managers not only have to manage how well caseworkers perform the eligibility function, they must also manage how well they perform the WTW function. While managing eligibility tasks is fairly straightforward (monitoring caseworker actions through auditing of caseworkers' case files), managing WTW tasks is more subtle. Some caseworker WTW actions (e.g., the timing of activities discussed in Section 4) can be monitored by checking the case file. For most WTW actions, however, there is no explicit book of regulations explaining what a caseworker should do to help a recipient achieve employment and welfare exit. Many of the actions (e.g., listening carefully to and encouraging the recipient, developing an appropriate WTW plan) are not recorded in the case file. It is therefore not possible for supervisors to manage WTW caseworkers by auditing case files to verify that correct (or even appropriate) actions were taken. However, while monitoring caseworker actions may not be feasible, supervisors can determine which caseworkers are placing more recipients in jobs and which caseworkers have more welfare exits. These "outcomes" of caseworkers' actions are observable and can be found in the case file.

*. . . which suggests a shift in management style.*

This analysis suggests a shift in management style—one that entails identifying appropriate outcomes, measuring those outcomes promptly and accurately, attributing them to a single individual or small group, and motivating workers to improve their performance as measured by the specified outcomes. Doing this in practice is difficult. It requires changes in worker culture and improvements in data systems. While almost all the counties have moved to a work-first, Job Club–centered program, few have made the corresponding transition to outcomes-based management. However, experience in GAIN and in the Job Training Partnership Act suggests that the payoff to doing so may be large.

## DEALING WITH NONCOMPLIANCE

One-third or more of those instructed to participate in an activity fail to do so. As noted above, noncompliance has many causes, ranging from CWD deficiencies to willful noncompliance, and home visits are a promising strategy to address the problem. Home visits, however, are time-consuming and to be done properly require specially trained staff. Many counties have pilot home visit programs in place or under development, but a universal home visit program—whether the visits are made immediately following noncompliance or after imposition of the sanction—would require the commitment of major resources. A multi-county randomized experiment to address this question is probably feasible and is worthy of serious consideration.

When counties determine that noncompliance is willful, they may impose sanctions. However, the current CalWORKs legislation does not allow CWDs to impose a full-family sanction for failure to participate in WTW activities under any circumstances; and in many counties, both senior management and caseworkers expressed concern that the statutory adult-only sanction itself is too small to have the desired effect of discouraging willful noncompliance. Whether counties should be given the option of a full-family sanction requires weighing two considerations: First, the effect of a full-family sanction on participation must be considered. While there are claims (from the state of Hawaii and from a recently suspended demonstration in San Mateo County) that full-family sanctions increase compliance, the formal evaluation evidence is mixed. Second, there are real concerns about the effects of a full-family sanction on the children the CalWORKs program is intended to protect. There are several ongoing studies of full-family sanctions, and as the results of those studies are released, the state could revisit the option of using such sanctions.

*An adult-only sanction may not be enough to discourage willful noncompliance.*

## POST-EMPLOYMENT SERVICES

Many participants have found jobs through Job Club and are working, but such jobs often do not pay enough to move recipients off aid and to self-sufficiency. Providing post-employment services, including more intensive case management and concurrent education and training, is part of the CalWORKs model.

Unfortunately, the limited evidence available on the success of such services is not very encouraging. The Riverside County GAIN results suggest that work-first alone is not enough to eventually get recipients off aid. Furthermore, a randomized trial of an intensive post-employment case management experiment (in Riverside County and in other counties nationwide) showed that such case management had no measurable effect on outcomes. In addition, concurrent education and training often appear impractical: A single mother raising a child (or several children) alone and working full time, often on an irregular work schedule, is not likely to be able to go back to school, especially if child care is not provided or is unavailable. Finally, many counties offering post-employment services report little recipient interest.

*Evidence on providing post-employment services is not encouraging.*

While some post-employment services are likely to be necessary to move recipients to self-sufficiency, more study is warranted, starting with identifying promising program models—for example, programs currently in some counties that encourage combining work and school—and rigorously evaluating them.

## CHILD CARE

*The current child-care system is cumbersome . . .*

The CalWORKs legislation established a cumbersome three-stage child-care system, with two different lead state agencies (CDSS and the California Department of Education), two different funding streams, and rules that sometimes varied with agency sponsorship. CDSS and the Department of Education have worked to improve the integration of the stages, but the current arrangement still has inconsistencies, and issues of coordination between the state agencies and county-level organizations have caused confusion and turmoil.

*. . . and raises equity issues.*

Beyond the problems with the existing three-stage system, there is also the relationship of CalWORKs to the broader child-care policy for the working poor. The current system gives higher priority for funding to current and recent CalWORKs recipients. Subsidizing all the working poor would be much more expensive than the current CalWORKs child-care system. The current child-care system (along with other CalWORKs services) also raises a serious equity issue: Why does the state offer child-care subsidies to all those who have been on aid, but to only a limited number of those who have not been on aid?

## BEHAVIORAL HEALTH

*Numbers of referrals have been much lower than expected.*

Although some analyses prior to CalWORKs projected that a large percentage of welfare recipients had serious substance abuse or mental health problems, referrals have been considerably lower than expected. There appear to be several reasons for this. First, the initial estimates of service needed may have been too high; second, those who may need treatment may be reluctant to self-identify because they are concerned about the involvement of child protective services in their case;

*Counties are moving to refine the program to achieve best outcomes.*

and third, CWD procedures are not always designed to elicit self-identification of behavioral health needs. Now, with more recipients reaching the assessment stage, more attention is being focused on this area, and several counties have procedures in place that appear worthy of careful consideration by other counties seeking to increase behavioral health referrals.

## FINAL THOUGHTS

As the implementation of CalWORKs moves into its third year, county programs enter a new phase. From a management perspective, counties can move from an emphasis on putting an initial program in place to an emphasis on refining the program to achieve the best possible outcomes. Doing so will often require a combination of program revisions, new approaches to management, and reworked computer and data systems.

Fortunately, CDSS and the counties begin work on these tasks from a solid base. The changed operating philosophy embodied in the CalWORKs legislation has stimulated real cultural change in CDSS and in the counties. Nevertheless, the task is daunting. Over the next few years, CDSS and the counties must show that their programs can continue to contribute to the caseload decline. Furthermore, they must do so quickly. For recipients, the 18-, 24-, and 60-month clocks are ticking. For the state as a whole and for the individual counties, the federal PRWORA legislation will be due for renewal in less than two years, and changes to California's CalWORKs legislation in reaction are also likely. It is too early to predict what changes will be enacted at renewal, but it seems likely that funding will be considerably tighter.

*Despite a solid base, the challenges are daunting.*

Thus, the next few years provide both challenges and opportunities. The CalWORKs program challenges CWDs to move participants through the steps of the CalWORKs model. CWDs and the state are also challenged to build an infrastructure to support the new work-first culture through appropriate performance-based management and computer systems.

*The next few years provide challenges. . .*

The CalWORKs program creates opportunities as well. How can welfare recipients be motivated to overcome their fears and take advantage of the program that one CWD employee described as a "once in a lifetime opportunity"? CWDs also have an opportunity to alter the way they do business. Funds are currently available to try new approaches and address important local issues. Over the next year, we will trace participant and agency responses to these challenges and opportunities as we return to our 24 study counties.

*. . . and opportunities.*